MAY 2001

D1409245

United States Presidents

Lyndon B. Johnson

Paul Joseph
ABDO Publishing Company

visit us at
www.abdopub.com

Published by ABDO Publishing Company 4940 Viking Drive, Edina, Minnesota 55435.
Copyright © 2000 by Abdo Consulting Group, Inc. International copyrights reserved in all countries. No part of this book may be reproduced in any form without written permission from the publisher.

Printed in the United States.

Photo credits: AP/Wide World, SuperStock, Archive, UPI/Corbis-Bettmann

Contributing editors: Robert Italia, Tamara L. Britton, K.M. Brielmaier, Kate A. Furlong

Library of Congress Cataloging-in-Publication Data

Joseph, Paul, 1970-
    Lyndon B. Johnson / Paul Joseph.
        p. cm. -- (United States presidents)
    Includes index.
    Summary: Traces the personal life and political career of the thirty-sixth president of the United States.
    ISBN 1-56239-814-8
    1. Johnson, Lyndon B. (Lyndon Baines), 1908-1973--Juvenile literature. 2. Presidents--United States--Biography--Juvenile literature. [1. Johnson, Lyndon B. (Lyndon Baines), 1908-1973. 2. Presidents.] I. Title. II. Series: United States presidents (Edina, Minn.)
E487.J67 1999
973.923'092--dc21
[B]   97-50200
                                                               CIP
                                                                AC

Contents

Lyndon B. Johnson

*A*t 2:38 P.M., on November 22, 1963, Lyndon B. Johnson was sworn in as the thirty-sixth president. It was unlike any other **inauguration**. The new president took the oath of office on the presidential plane, Air Force One.

Less than two hours earlier, President John F. Kennedy had died in Dallas, Texas. He had been shot while riding in a **motorcade** through downtown Dallas. Johnson, riding two cars behind Kennedy, was unhurt.

The entire nation was in shock over the loss of its president. When Air Force One landed in Washington, D.C., Johnson delivered his first official words as president: "This is a sad time for all people. We have suffered a loss that cannot be weighed. . . . I will do my best. That is all I can do. I ask for your help—and God's."

Johnson carried out many of John Kennedy's plans for America. But he could not bring an end to the **Vietnam War**. Johnson did not seek re-election. Instead, he retired to his ranch. He died on January 22, 1973.

Lyndon B. Johnson

Lyndon B. Johnson (1908-1973)
Thirty-sixth President

BORN:	August 27, 1908
PLACE OF BIRTH:	Near Stonewall, Texas
ANCESTRY:	British
FATHER:	Samuel Ealy Johnson, Jr., (1877-1937)
MOTHER:	Rebekah Baines Johnson (1881-1958)
WIFE:	Claudia Alta "Lady Bird" Taylor (1912-)
CHILDREN:	Two girls
EDUCATION:	Johnson City High School, Southwest Texas State Teachers College, Georgetown University Law School
RELIGION:	Disciples of Christ
OCCUPATION:	School teacher, rancher
MILITARY SERVICE:	Lieutenant commander and commander in the U.S. Naval Reserve
POLITICAL PARTY:	Democrat

OFFICES HELD:	National Youth Administration director in Texas, member of U.S. House of Representatives, U.S. senator, vice president
AGE AT INAUGURATION:	55
YEARS SERVED:	1963-1969
VICE PRESIDENT:	Hubert Humphrey
DIED:	January 22, 1973, San Antonio, Texas, age 64
CAUSE OF DEATH:	Heart attack

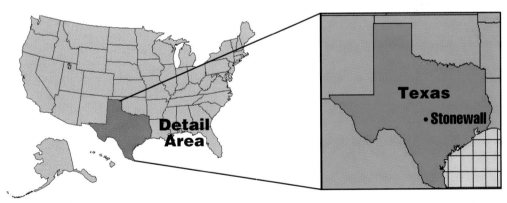

Birthplace of Lyndon Johnson

Growing Up
in Johnson City

*L*yndon Baines Johnson was born on August 27, 1908, on a small farm near Stonewall, Texas. He was the oldest of five children born to Sam Ealy Johnson, Jr., and Rebekah Baines Johnson.

When Lyndon was five years old, his family moved to Johnson City, Texas. His grandfather was one of the first settlers of the town and it was named after him.

Lyndon did odd jobs to help support the family. He shined shoes in the barbershop and herded goats for ranchers.

Lyndon was an average student in school. He was known more for his leadership skills. In 1924, he graduated from high school. His parents wanted him to go to college. But he didn't think he needed to.

Lyndon and some friends headed to California. He worked odd jobs but didn't make enough money for food. Hungry and homesick, he returned to Johnson City. He was ready for college.

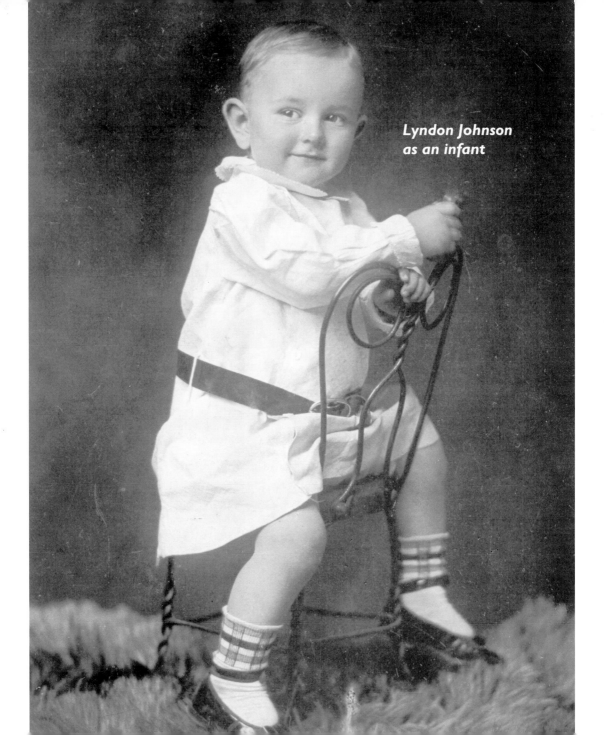

Lyndon Johnson
as an infant

College, Teaching, and Lady Bird

*J*ohnson borrowed some money and set out for Southwest Texas State Teachers College in San Marcos, Texas. He worked part-time jobs to help pay for school.

Johnson could not make enough money to meet his expenses. He had to borrow from friends and relatives. In 1928, he left school for a year to earn some money. He got a temporary job teaching at Welhausen Grade School in Cotulla, Texas.

In 1929, Johnson returned to college. He graduated in 1930. From there he went to Houston. There, he taught public speaking and coached the debate team at Sam Houston High School. He also began working on Congressman Richard M. Kleberg's election campaign.

After Johnson had taught for a year, Congressman Kleberg offered him a job. Johnson moved to Washington, D.C. He worked as Kleberg's personal secretary.

In 1934, Johnson met Claudia Alta Taylor and quickly fell in love. Within two months they were married.

Claudia came from a wealthy family. When Claudia was a baby, she was nicknamed "Lady Bird." Her nanny had said she was as pretty as a ladybird.

Lyndon and Lady Bird had two daughters. Lynda Bird was born in 1944. Luci Baines was born in 1947.

In 1943, Lady Bird bought a radio station, KTBC. She started a company called the Texas Broadcasting Company. Lady Bird bought several more radio and television stations. She changed the name of her company to the LBJ Company.

The LBJ Company became very successful. The company also bought a bank and property. The Johnsons became very wealthy.

Lyndon and Lady Bird Johnson

11

Politics and World War II

*I*n 1935, Lyndon Johnson was appointed director of the National Youth Administration in Texas by President Franklin D. Roosevelt. Johnson set up programs to keep young children in school. He created work-study jobs to help students pay for college. And he created training classes for young people who needed skills to get jobs.

In 1937, Johnson was elected to the United States **House of Representatives**. There, Johnson worked to bring electricity to Texans who lived in the country. He also set up projects to build dams, irrigate farms, and give loans to farmers. And Johnson helped start many job and relief programs in Texas.

On December 7, 1941, the Japanese attacked Pearl Harbor in Hawaii. America entered **World War II**. Johnson became the first congressman to serve in the war. For his bravery during the war, Johnson received the Silver Star Medal.

Johnson returned to **Congress** in July 1942. He argued for more aid and supplies for soldiers fighting in the war. In 1943, Johnson was a member of the Naval Affairs Committee. He and his staff made sure the navy used its resources effectively.

In 1947, Johnson voted for the Taft-Hartley Act. This law protected workers' rights to organize in unions and bargain with their employers. It also protected employers against strikes that would cause national emergencies or break contracts. Johnson served five full terms in the U.S. **House of Representatives**. In 1948, he ran for the U.S. Senate and won.

In the Senate, Johnson supported government help for the elderly and disabled. He also supported education and higher wages for workers. Johnson soon became a **Democratic** party leader. He was re-elected in 1954.

Johnson suffered a heart attack in 1955. Four months later, he returned to the Senate. In 1957, Johnson helped pass a **civil rights** bill. It was the first one passed since 1875. On April 14, 1958, he helped create a bill that formed the National Aeronautics and Space Administration (NASA). In 1959, Johnson quit his Senate seat. He wanted to be president.

Congressman Lyndon Johnson

Vice President Johnson

*I*n 1960, Johnson campaigned for the **Democratic** presidential nomination. But the Democrats chose John F. Kennedy to run for president. They chose Johnson as Kennedy's vice-presidential running mate.

Kennedy and Johnson made a good team. Kennedy was from the North while Johnson was from the South. Northerners and Southerners voted for them. Kennedy and Johnson won the election.

Johnson was an active vice president. He attended cabinet meetings and special White House meetings. Johnson was the chairman of the President's Committee on Equal Employment Opportunity. This group wanted to end racial **discrimination** in the workplace.

Vice President Johnson also headed the National Advisory Council for the Peace Corps. The Peace Corps is a group of American volunteers that go to developing countries to teach people about health, agriculture, and education.

In November 1963, Kennedy and Johnson started to campaign for the 1964 election. One stop was Johnson's home state of Texas.

On November 22, 1963, President Kennedy was shot while riding in the backseat of a car driving through downtown Dallas. Johnson waited at the hospital while doctors tried to save President Kennedy's life. When Kennedy was pronounced dead, Johnson boarded Air Force One to return to Washington, D.C. On the plane, Lyndon Baines Johnson was sworn in as the thirty-sixth president.

Lyndon Johnson is sworn in as president after John F. Kennedy's assassination. Mrs. Jacqueline Kennedy is on the right.

The Making of the Thirty-sixth United States President

1908
Born August 27 in Stonewall, Texas

1913
The family moves to Johnson City, Texas

1924
Graduates from high school

1930
Graduates from Southwest Texas State Teachers College

1935
Becomes director of the National Youth Administration of Texas

1937
Elected to the U.S. House of Representatives

1941
Lieutenant Commander for the Navy in WWII

1948
Elected to the United States Senate

1953
Elected minority leader in the Senate

1959
Resigns from Senate

1960
Elected vice president under John F. Kennedy

1963
Kennedy assassinated; Johnson takes oath of office

1964
Civil Rights Bill passes; elected president

PRESIDENTIAL

Lyndon B. Johnson

"If we fail now, then we will have forgotten in abundance what we learned in hardship: that democracy rests on faith . . ."

➤ **1931**
Teaches at Sam Houston High School

➤ **1932**
Becomes secretary to Congressman Richard M. Kleberg

➤ **1934**
Marries Claudia Alta "Lady Bird" Taylor on November 17

Historic Events
during Johnson's Presidency

★ Earthquake in Alaska measures 8.5 on the Richter Scale

★ Chemists at Stanford University produce synthetic DNA

★ Aswan High Dam on Egypt's Nile River is completed

➤ **1954**
Re-elected to Senate

➤ **1955**
Suffers a heart attack; elected Senate majority leader

➤ **1957**
Passes civil rights bill

1965
Inaugurated on January 20

1968
Decides not to run for a second term; Nixon elected president

1969
Retires to his ranch in Texas

➤ **1973**
Dies on January 22

YEARS

The Thirty-sixth President

*I*n the weeks after Kennedy's death, Johnson helped calm the nation. He showed strong leadership, and worked with **Congress** to pass important laws.

On July 2, 1964, President Johnson signed the historic **Civil Rights** Act. It banned **discrimination** in public places. It pushed for **desegregation** of schools. And it held back money from agencies, schools, and businesses that practiced discrimination.

Johnson worked on laws that would help the poor and give more money to schools. Johnson also signed the biggest tax cut in U.S. history. By now, most of Kennedy's policies were passed. Johnson began working on his own policies.

But there was trouble in Asia. Back in 1954, Vietnam was divided in two. North Vietnam was **Communist**. South Vietnam was a **democracy**. Elections were planned in 1956 to reunite the countries. But the leader of South Vietnam, Ngo Dinh Diem, refused to participate in the elections. He did not want Vietnam to be a communist country.

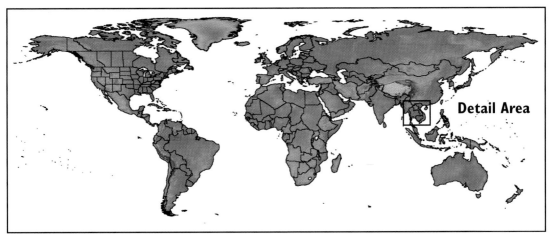

Detail Area

China

North
Vietnam

Burma

Laos

*Gulf of
Tonkin*

Thailand

Cambodia

South
Vietnam

SOUTHEAST ASIA
during the Vietnam War

North Vietnam attacked South Vietnam in 1956. America supported South Vietnam because it was anti-**communist**. Both President Eisenhower and President Kennedy sent money and military advisers to help South Vietnam.

On August 2, 1964, North Vietnamese ships attacked an American navy ship, the USS *Maddox,* in the Gulf of Tonkin. On August 7, **Congress** passed the Tonkin Gulf Resolution. It gave President Johnson the power to "repel any armed attack" by North Vietnam. Johnson started sending American troops to Vietnam to help fight the war.

American soldiers in South Vietnam

Lyndon Johnson visits American troops in Vietnam.

The Seven "Hats" of the U.S. President

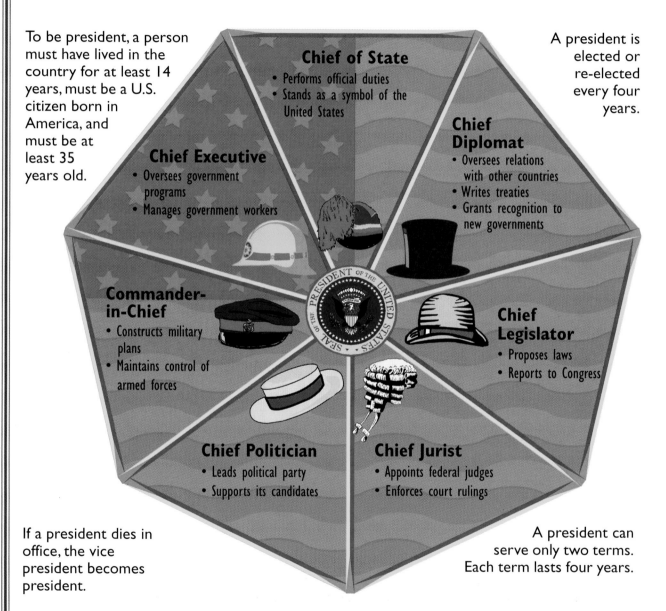

To be president, a person must have lived in the country for at least 14 years, must be a U.S. citizen born in America, and must be at least 35 years old.

A president is elected or re-elected every four years.

Chief of State
- Performs official duties
- Stands as a symbol of the United States

Chief Diplomat
- Oversees relations with other countries
- Writes treaties
- Grants recognition to new governments

Chief Executive
- Oversees government programs
- Manages government workers

Commander-in-Chief
- Constructs military plans
- Maintains control of armed forces

Chief Legislator
- Proposes laws
- Reports to Congress

Chief Politician
- Leads political party
- Supports its candidates

Chief Jurist
- Appoints federal judges
- Enforces court rulings

If a president dies in office, the vice president becomes president.

A president can serve only two terms. Each term lasts four years.

As president, Lyndon Johnson had seven jobs.

The Three Branches of the U.S. Government

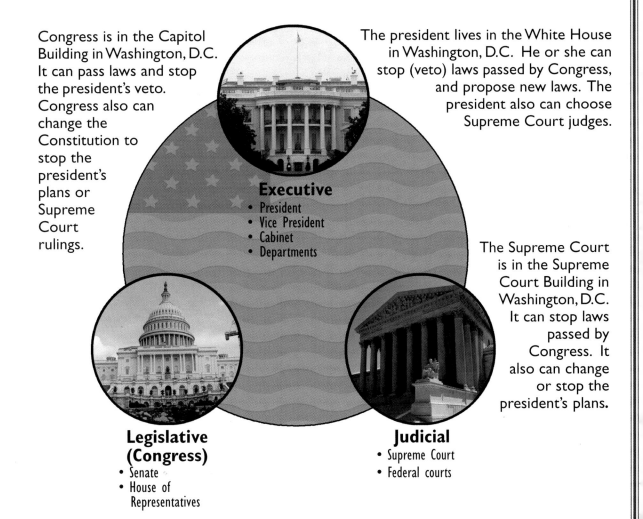

Congress is in the Capitol Building in Washington, D.C. It can pass laws and stop the president's veto. Congress also can change the Constitution to stop the president's plans or Supreme Court rulings.

The president lives in the White House in Washington, D.C. He or she can stop (veto) laws passed by Congress, and propose new laws. The president also can choose Supreme Court judges.

Executive
- President
- Vice President
- Cabinet
- Departments

The Supreme Court is in the Supreme Court Building in Washington, D.C. It can stop laws passed by Congress. It also can change or stop the president's plans.

Legislative (Congress)
- Senate
- House of Representatives

Judicial
- Supreme Court
- Federal courts

The U.S. Constitution formed three government branches. Each branch has power over the others. So, no single group or person can control the country. The Constitution calls this "separation of powers."

The Great Society

*I*n November 1964, Lyndon Johnson was elected president. At the time, he won the greatest election victory in U.S. history.

On January 20, 1965, Johnson was **inaugurated** for his first full term as president. He spoke of his dream to "end poverty and racial injustice." He called his plans the Great Society.

Johnson started his programs immediately. Medicare gave money to the elderly in need of medical care. Head Start helped poor children get ready for school. And Job Corps helped train youths so they could get better jobs.

Johnson signed the Voting Rights Act of 1965. This bill made sure African Americans had an equal chance to vote. He said, "This bill is not just about voting rights for blacks, but really it's about all of us who must overcome the crippling legacy of bigotry and injustice."

President Johnson led the way for **civil rights**. In January 1966, Johnson named Robert C. Weaver the secretary of Housing and Urban Development (HUD). Weaver was the first African American to head a cabinet department. In 1967,

Johnson appointed the first African American Supreme Court Justice, Thurgood Marshall.

But the war in Vietnam was going badly. Even with American troops, South Vietnam was struggling. The North Vietnamese had help from China, which was also a **Communist** country. And many South Vietnamese people favored the North. They used **guerrilla warfare** to fight American and South Vietnamese soldiers.

President Johnson deep in thought at the White House, 1968

President Johnson sent more and more troops to help South Vietnam. There were almost 400,000 Americans in Vietnam by 1967. Many thousands died. Soon, Americans began protesting the war. Johnson's popularity fell quickly.

By early 1968, Johnson had realized that it was almost impossible to win the war. On March 31, he announced a pause in the bombing of North Vietnam and the opening of peace talks. He also said that he would not run for president in 1968.

Back to the Ranch

*J*anuary 20, 1969, was President Johnson's last day as president. He and Lady Bird retired to their ranch in Texas.

The Johnsons built a presidential library and museum and an addition at the University of Texas at Austin. Johnson also wrote a book about his presidency, entitled *The Vantage Point.*

Johnson died of a heart attack on January 22, 1973. Three days later, the **Vietnam War** ended.

As president, Lyndon Johnson served his country well. He showed strong leadership after John Kennedy's **assassination**. He signed into law the most important **civil rights** acts since the **Civil War**. And he started important social services programs. He is also remembered for his part in the American tragedy known as the Vietnam War.

Opposite page: Lyndon Johnson at the LBJ Ranch

Fun Facts

- Johnson was the second tallest president, at six feet, three inches. Abraham Lincoln was taller by only one inch.

- The initials "LBJ" stood for the entire Johnson family: Lyndon Baines Johnson; his wife, Lady Bird Johnson; and his daughters, Lynda Bird Johnson and Luci Baines Johnson.

- President Johnson had the nickname "Light Bulb" Johnson because he would turn off lights in unoccupied rooms of the White House. Johnson did not want to waste electricity and taxpayers' money. Many staff members who left their offices often returned to dark rooms.

- LBJ once had a Texas barbecue on the roof of the White House. He served steak, baked potatoes, corn pudding, and pecan pie.

Opposite page: LBJ playing with his dogs on the White House lawn

Glossary

assassinate - to murder a very important person.

civil rights - the rights of every U.S. citizen.

Civil War - 1861-1865. A war between the Union and the Confederate States of America.

communism - a system where everything is run and owned by the state and given to people as they need it. It was seen as a threat because the Soviet Union, a communist nation, was an enemy of the U.S. after World War II.

Congress - the lawmaking body of a nation. It is made up of the Senate and the House of Representatives.

democracy - a system where citizens vote to decide how the country should be run.

Democrat - one of the two main political parties in the United States. Democrats are often liberal and believe in more government.

desegregation - making things open to all people no matter their race.

discrimination - when someone is treated badly because of his or her race.

guerilla warfare - when people fight in small groups using unusual tactics, such as terrorism and sabotage.

House of Representatives - a group of people elected by citizens to represent them. They meet in Washington, D.C., and make laws for the nation.

inaugurate - to swear someone into office.

motorcade - a parade of cars or motorcycles.

Vietnam War - 1955-1975. A long, failed attempt by the U.S. to help keep South Vietnam from being taken over by Communist North Vietnam.

World War II - 1939 to 1945, fought in Europe, Asia, and Africa. The United States, France, Great Britain, the Soviet Union, and their allies were on one side. Germany, Italy, Japan, and their allies were on the other side. The war began when Germany invaded Poland. America entered the war in 1941 after Japan bombed Pearl Harbor, Hawaii.

Internet Sites

The Presidents of the United States of America
http://www.whitehouse.gov/WH/glimpse/presidents/html/presidents.html
This site is from the White House. With an introduction from President Bill Clinton and biographies that include each president's inaugural address, this site is excellent. Get information on White House history, art in the White House, first ladies, first families, and much more.

POTUS—Presidents of the United States
http://www.ipl.org/ref/POTUS/
In this resource you will find background information, election results, cabinet members, presidency highlights, and some odd facts on each of the presidents. Links to biographies, historical documents, audio and video files, and other presidential sites are also included to enrich this site.

These sites are subject to change. Go to your favorite search engine and type in United States presidents for more sites.

Pass It On

History enthusiasts: educate readers around the country by passing on information you've learned about presidents or other important people who've changed history. Share your little-known facts and interesting stories. We want to hear from you!

To get posted on the ABDO Publishing Company Web site, email us at:
history@abdopub.com
Visit the ABDO Publishing Company Web site at www.abdopub.com

Index